Lost Futures: Imagined Ends

Lost Futures: Imagined Ends

Avarithia

*"It is what we wish we had not lost the most
that makes us truly Human" — Avarithia*

To Mary Ann

and

Martin M

and

To all that could have been

Disclaimer

Lost Futures: Imagined Ends is a hybrid work of poetry. The writings are born from the author's imagination and lived experiences, deliberately blurred and reshaped. While inspired by universal themes such as loss and recovery. Any resemblance to actual individuals or events is purely coincidental. This book was written entirely by the author, with minor grammar and style edits assisted by Grammarly's non-generative tools. All content remains the original work of the author.

Contents

Lost Futures

Imagined Ends

Preface

This book serves as the headstone for the burial site of many potential futures where this text may not have otherwise come into existence. This book is an admission of the Human mind's frantic logical grasping for control in the face of loss. And the mind's attempts to mitigate pain while processing the unstoppable losses that arise throughout Human experience.

In this text, over sixty poems highlight loss in various forms. Themes of love and survival are prevalent throughout these poems, which lay bare the vulnerability and strength that connect Humanity. Each poem pays respect to loss and every attempt to heal. From gut-wrenching stories to the Human imagination and also more specific states of mind. *Lost Futures: Imagined Ends* is the light that says, "Keep going," "You are not alone," and "There is always another way," a collection to inspire hope.

This poetic journey presents readers with a mixture of poems. Showcasing the movement from hopeless, devastating loss to transformation and healing. This book comprises two main sections, *Lost Futures* and *Imagined Ends*. The focus of *Lost Futures* is loss. The focus of *Imagined Ends* is transformation and healing. Both sections' themes bleed into each other, but their sequence is intentional. Outlining the heavy experience of loss before reaching brighter outcomes.

Lost Futures: Imagined Ends: the poetic exploration of the challenges, coping, and healing arising after loss. Humanity has the resilience to heal from painful losses. This book provides insight into a beautiful side of Humanity. Their compassion for loss and their triumphs, endurance, and imagination to survive beyond loss.

Thank you for choosing this book. I hope it helps you live beyond lost futures. May this book bring you happiness, peace, and better ends.

Author's Note

The pen name Avarithia is an alteration of a similar name I created many years ago. I had been immersed in occult books when I made it. Later, I read heavily into psychology. Avarithia appeared shortly after. I felt that Ava, the feminine element in the name, was purposeful. The latter part of the pen name adds some weight and mystery. There's a depth to the name that I like. I decided on this pen name as a compensatory creative persona. I chose this pen name with the hope and intention of writing many books in the future!

This book is my first. Some of this book's content is older poems of mine that I found suited the themes. It took two months to write the rest. I have inserted some content before the main sections as groundwork for the rest of the book. That content gives examples of what will follow throughout, giving the reader a starting point for this intended journey of loss towards healing.

For editing purposes, I have crafted this book with intentionally uncommon edits. The poems feature both left and right-aligned text. Read the poems in line order from the top of the page to the bottom of the page. Take less regard for the text alignment. I have been capitalizing every "Human" in the book for their importance and distinction. This book is a dedication to all that Humanity is and can be despite loss. I felt it fitting to highlight "Human" out of respect for the themes. There is a neologism in the poem *Sleeping Rough*. The word is "Grateciation," which is a combination of gratitude and appreciation. A word that combined the meanings of both did not exist, so I made one.

This book tackles individual loss. But there are higher implications. Humanity has so much potential, but death haunts every moment. It steals futures from us. We let our moments go too easily. They pass us by. What could've been dies and fades away into eternity. I hope that by exploring the tragedy of loss, beautiful changes may occur. How we treat each moment could be different. We have the opportunity to change.

There's so much death for us in life. But there's also so much beauty and meaning in being alive. It is a shame that we get damaged by loss. I hope this book can help mend some of those wounds. All I wanted to do was create something beautiful. I hope that this book can move people emotionally, inspire change in their lives, or have a positive effect on their imagination. If this book creates brighter futures, then I am happy.

This project really was a labour of love. As you may realise by the time you finish reading, I too have been impacted by loss in my life. Even though it has been difficult, I have always maintained a feeling that, although everything is shrouded in darkness, there is always light out there. I learned that this is not a passive process; the light is out there, but I have to reach for it, and I have. Many moments are filled with grateciation now. The simple beauty of our being alive falls through the cracks of our perception. May this book inspire people to live fuller, happier lives. And also may their perception of life expand. So they may experience its beauty.

— Avarithia

Introduction

I knew that preparing for eventual loss in life would act as a buffer for me in the future. Life is so unpredictable; it felt right to prepare myself for any eventuality. Loss is not an easy topic to write about, but the role that loss has played in my life has been significant. It has been devastating, transformative, and renewing. I needed to write about it.

In the past, I saw life through a dark and narrow lens. It is different now. Out of all the loss I experienced, beauty emerged. Every day leads to more understanding and insight. Loss and the grief that comes with it touched my heart. The purpose of this book is to highlight the beauty that survives loss. That even with loss and grief, life goes on, and so do you.

Loss and life have meaning. Both transform the way we understand our lives. Part of the reason for writing this book is to show that the meanings we create can have a positive or negative impact on us. This impact is a significant point that I have incorporated into the poetry. We can come away from a loss destroyed, stagnant, or focused on moving on with our lives.

I wanted to show that there are positive outcomes beyond loss. There is a strong sense of hope. I originally planned to write an entirely sad book about loss. But I really could not talk about loss without mentioning the beautiful meanings that we create out of love and to survive.

Ultimately, I decided to show both the dark and the light sides of loss. The journey of this book begins with experiencing loss and then undergoing a process of healing and creating beautiful meanings. Thus, arriving at gratitude and appreciation for yourself, life, and the people you love.

The first main section of the book *Lost Futures* includes poems about death with negative endings. The magnitude of these poems helps build towards the second section of the book. Some of the poems have a purely melancholic feeling. While others are sad, they have some beauty attached to them.

There's a strong sense of hopelessness in *Lost Futures*. If I were to release this book with just this section, it would still cover both the light and dark aspects of loss. However, the book would not feel complete without the following section. Adding *Imagined Ends* brings this work full circle in a positive sense.

The second main section, *Imagined Ends*, brings a change of tone. Coming out of the devastation of loss. This section represents the transformation of the self along that journey. Moving from the initial grief of loss, through mourning, into healing. Overcoming loss and its challenges. The integration of loss into one's life in a positive way.

This section is more optimistic and has better outcomes. Resilience and beauty are noticeable in many of the poems. Loss is the starting place of a long journey that imagined ends emerge from. We live, continuing to imagine new futures and outcomes for ourselves despite loss. We are not lost futures; we can have lost futures. May this book give you hope or the will to imagine better ends for yourself, regardless of the losses you face.

Just like life, where you cannot be sure what you will receive. The poems in this book are in their original order. Light and dark throughout. I am happy that even if I were to arrange them perfectly, it would not be as meaningful to me as the original sequence of their creation. Keep this in mind as you experience the entire book. You are moving through loss, into recovery, reaching beautiful meanings!

Before the main content of the book, I have prepared some introductory content that will be of interest to you. The first writing is a dream I had many years ago. I had experienced a lot within a few years; this dream resulted from much loss. It is titled *A Scary Dream*. Following this dream, the first poem, titled *I Left Him by the Door to the Ocean,* is sure to grab your attention.

A Scary Dream

Here is a dream I had back in March 2022. I have been able to apply this to different areas of my life. The symbolism is strong. Its effect was moving. The emotional release from the emergence of this dream was immense. The dream follows below,

I was in a mansion. I walked out the door, closing it behind me. Out the back onto a long descending rectangular garden. I walked down the descending garden lawn. It was sunny. On the bottom left of the garden, there stood a destroyed mansion. Abandoned and overgrown with plants, bushes, trees, and weeds, with no windows or doors.

Walking past the front of the abandoned mansion. I turned left and walked around the right side, walking through an archway of gigantic trees. They seemed cut. The tree branches had spiked ends. They looked like snakes. I walked past the side of the mansion under the tall trees to a graveyard to the left, out the back of the building, along the straight path. The large trees stood over the graves below. Attached to the underside of these trees were female statues.

Strolling to the end of the path. I looked up at all these large female statues above me on these trees as I passed. They were under the branches, eyes closed, facing downwards. The statues were of white marble. Women, maybe goddesses. They had long hair and wore white dresses. They held unidentified objects. The statues were somehow attached to the tree branches.

I walked past the line of large trees with the female statues. Turning left at the end of the path. I walked upwards, ascending the pathway. I passed the side of the small graveyard. As I reached the top of the path, I had a strong intuition that something was going to fall. I reached the top of the path, and there were more graves. I turned left onto a path, which would lead me back to the garden I had come from. I saw that opening in the bushes in the distance.

On my left, there was a large tree. There was a grave below it. Above the grave was a branch. Pinned to the branch was a female statue. Just ahead of this large tree, there were three graves with oval gravestone heads. On my right, there was a raised, straight dirt mound the whole way along the path. On top of the mound, there was a line of bushes, trees, and shrubs.

Standing at the top of the path I'd just come up to, I noticed the surrounding area. I walked past the tree, statue, and grave. These were behind me now. I walked towards the other graves with the oval heads. Heads carved out of stone. They had hollow eye sockets. No eyes. The oval heads with their hollow sockets looked upwards. Before I could walk any further towards them, something happened.

The statue attached to the tree behind me fell. It fell and crashed through the thick, large gravestone with a loud crash. It fell out of sight into the grave below. The crash shocked me. I had turned around in terror, fright, and I had fallen backwards onto the ground and screamed. I could feel, sense, and perceive the terror and shock that this caused me. Although intuition previously alerted me. I was still shocked and surprised by what had happened.

I could feel a force behind my body, close to me. Another force's presence. I felt it pass over me and move overhead in the direction of the fallen statue. The feeling scared me; it made me panic more. The statue of the woman had crashed straight into the grave. Breaking the gravestone. The crash had sent stone flying in every direction. I had put my open hand, palm out, like a sort of banishing ritual towards the open grave. Towards the statue in the grave. Like protection from the statue.

After I had done this for a few seconds, I recovered from the shock. I looked towards the headstones. All the headstones, eerily, had turned to look at me. All were facing me, looking straight at me. Eyeless. Their focus unsettled me deeply. It was unsettling. A piece of the gravestone lay near me. This stone had landed at the base of my left foot. It was black, circular, and a little bigger than the palm of my hand. I was still in the position I had fallen to in fright. I looked upon the stone. It had circular, sharp curves. It was shiny on top.

Dream Note

I quote from my notes about this dream: "I was upset by the dream. But I had no idea why this had such a huge impact on me. I just kept crying. I was calm but upset. It felt like something unknown was pouring out of me, all by itself. I can't explain how distinctly separate these two states were, simultaneously. Calmness, and yet, I was outpouring emotion. Still mind and releasing emotion."

The symbolic journey of the dream is transferable. I have applied it to many aspects of my life. It shows the beginning of a loss.

I Left Him by the Door to the Ocean

This poem highlights a dark transformation of the mind. When all hope is lost, the mind finds a way to cope. Unfortunately, sometimes it is too late. Even when near the end, there is hope for peace of mind and change. In most cases, it does not need to get so severe for meanings and the mind to change. But sometimes tragedies occur.

Written in July 2025 after I experienced my own form of transformed mind. The poem follows below,

I broke the waves,
And they crashed,
To the floor; around me,
Flowing away in red.

Nausea, as I drifted away,
From the shore,
Time slows on this fall,
Peacefully.

To rest,
At the bottom of the ocean,
I reached it,
Drenched in the red.

I can't feel it anymore,
No separation,
Between each wave,
All one sea,
The sea of me.

The most peaceful way to drown,
It is in yourself quietly,
Over time.

The seabed consumed me,
I consumed myself,
Was it me who did it?
Through some eyes,
Maybe my own.

Clearer,
They see me now,
See what I left behind at the bottom,
As I wipe off the blood,
Sitting up on the floor,
Getting up to walk away.

Those eyes see me,
Her eyes see me,
The shock,
As I appear before her,
The person she loved,
Changed.

I wipe off his blood,
Walk towards her,
And she retracts,
Then she realises,
It's me.

We both recognise each other,
We recognise ourselves,
That perfect embrace,
Of oneself,
After birth, through death.

Then it reverses,
Back to where I was before,
Before he died,
Back in the trap,
Before he drowned,
Back to being broken,
Before being lost in the sea,
The sea of me.

Lost in the darkness,
Heavy in existence,
Back-to-back, back-to-before,
With my demons,
Supported and poisoned,
By my lies and my needs.

The venom in the veins,
The lack of feeling,
Numb, by being pushed,
Held just beneath the water,
Perpetual darkened bliss,
Before the shock.

The truth of what I am,
And what I believed,
I would die again,
And again, and again,
And again, to embrace with you,
The ember of death is worth.

Scared so much,
I couldn't do it,
But for you, I would die again,
Let me die again,
Die again, die again,
And again, for you,
Love.

Go back and see,
The real ocean with me,
Now that we've found each other,
And found each other in ourselves,
I'd die for you, as I died in the sea of me,
No longer do I separate,
I see you, and in turn, I see me,
I love you.

Cop 1: "It was suicide; the cut marks on the appendage."
Cop 2: "No... seems it was an accident."
Cop 2: "Trying to bandage himself."
Cop 2: "Cut himself badly and collapsed."
Cop 1: "What a shame."

xxx

Staring at the open, cold eyes,
Of the injured man, dead on the floor,
In this lonely kitchen,
The recently abandoned family home.

Cop 2: "A family lived here previously."
Cop 2: "That was the husband."
Woman: "I know."

Poem Note

In this layered poem, tragedy collides with success. Transformation occurs in the mind of the man. Overcoming mental obstacles that burden the mind. The late feelings and understanding of the man's relationship issues come to the fore. Revelations unknown to others. In this tragic loss. The preciousness and importance of life are shown in the last moments as it fades away into cold, lifeless darkness. Never to be fully understood or shared with others. The witnessing of the death of love.

I Left Him by the Door to the Ocean presents the importance of the theme of *Lost Futures*. And the mind's manufacturing of imagined ends. The emphasis here is that we want to create better ends, not tragedies. Now moving on to the first main section. Further observation of lost futures and the mind.

Lost Futures

I Watched Her Slow, Silent Explosion

Locked, focus,
Down, came the Moon,
Angelic flames,
Lipstick fumes.

In the street,
As I drove by,
Came to a halt,
Teary-eyed.

A slow, silent explosion,
No fuss,
Transformational ashes,
Watching was rough.

I arrived home,
Turning the key,
Sat by the table,
Crying eerily.

Earth,
Lost the Moon,
This angel,
Struck the match.

Never seen beauty,
Cause attention,
So fast.

Why had the Moon resorted,
To a volcanic clash?
Pompe display,
Descending, no attempt could catch.

Why, oh why,
Did the lovely Moon,
Burnout?
Burst like a balloon.

I wish I'd stopped her,
Before she'd ignite,
Safe from falling,
To live, delight.

This darkness,
The surrounding plume,
Hidden pain,
Escaped doom.

I wish,
She was still alive,
Could've helped,
Could've tried.

Now the world,
Has lost the Moon,
Sealing itself,
In the dark side's gloom.

If she survived,
Would I have cared?
Listened, heard,
"She was scared."

It's too late,
She is gone,
My grief for her,
Lives on.

My Brother Harold

Dog walking,
On a winter's night,
Harold and I,
Enjoyed the stars in sight.

> Crossing the bridge,
> Close to home,
> The local gang,
> Surrounded us,
> On their roam.

Harold,
Stopped wagging his tail,
As the louts pounced,
Our backs to the rail.

> Taking the tags,
> From my Harold's neck,
> Swooping him up,
> Over the rail he went.

Not a moment had passed,
I went over, be-hind,
To save him,
The others, not so kind.

Carried, drifted, swirling away,
A war of currents,
Living decay,
A deceased tree,
Reached out its hand,
Grabbing us both,
In a way, I did not understand.

For poor Harold,
It was too late,
The water left him,
In a desperate state.

Exhausted,
I tried to lift,
Drenched in water,
Frozen, moved no bit.

Struggling brought him,
Up to my chest, through snow,
To the roadside,
"Harold!" I went.

By chance?
The sheriff drove by,
Leaping out of the cruiser,
Shock in the eye.

"My dear, don't cry,"
Towels and foil,
Wrapped,
Harold and I.

At the station,
My mother arrived,
Rushing to me,
"You could've died!"

I said to the officer,
"When can I see him?"
Ushering my mother,
Couldn't hear.

Told shortly after,
Harold was dead,
The monsters had taken him,
The river, they fed.

Asked me, "What happened?"
The louts, gang, and bridge,
"Dramatic events,
For a bunch of kids."

In the morning,
To my surprise,
Dog tags lay,
At my bedside.

It seemed,
When I explained,
Officers arrested,
Evidence, they obtained.

Harold and I went through a war,
Brothers, a bond no one could ignore,
Harold put to rest,
My brother's name tag retrieved,
I'd done my best,
Had my Harold seen?

Years passed,
I want Harold here with me,
My fifteen-year-old brother,
I know he misses me.

Conflicted are my Romantic Blues

"Make your way to me."

How could I do that?

"It's easy, don't you see?"

Crushed under your weighted "spat."

"This is how it needs to be."

You are the only person telling me that.

So far away,
Gave up in time,
Where was your effort?
Focused solely on mine.

Left me ashamed,
Blamed,
Failings like stains,
Rupturing brains.

I am stuck,
You are free,
Living your life,
Happily,
What about me?

Long distance,
Cutting the threads,
You married your husband,
Ruptures again.

"You didn't have the money,
Baby, you failed,
Couldn't do enough,
That ship has sailed."

Expected our life,
I was wrong,
Couldn't trust you,
The hurt, love is gone.

Frozen heart,
In orbit,
Passing over me.

Brain,
Turned noodles,
Chronic,
TV.

Why, why let go of me?

"So easily."

You wanted me dead?

"That is a fact."

You never said so.

                              "It required no single act."

The time wasted,
Pandering to you.

                                   "I played you."

Turned into a broken tune.

                              What's left to say,
                              You were my disease,
                              Working on a cure,
                              To feel at ease.

Wanted our life so badly,
Forgot my needs,
I recognise now,
What's important to me.

                              Took time,
                              To be healthy,
                              When you left,
                              My life.

Your immature actions,
Threats with a knife,
The end brought by,
Intuitive foresight.

                              Horror show,
                              Romantic blues,
                              Wasn't love,
                              Lies emanating from you.

"Got divorced,
I'd love to see you,
Booked the flights."

                                       There's no chance,
                                         I'll be near you.

Marionette no Strings

Feelings, deranged,
Marionette no strings,
Collapsed building,
Needle, syringe.

Twinge, the book's spine,
Pages, losing their bind,
Sprawled, all over the floor,
Numb, words ignored.

Horrible,
Lasting,
Mistake.

Soft,
As a freshly baked cake,
Stringed motion,
One cannot make.

Protect me, protect me not,
Blame myself, degenerative rot.

Choices like lead,
Debt, tooth be filled,
Health gone malignant,
No drop of blood spilled.

Unnecessary losses,
Application, pills,
Trapped in a nightmare,
Goodbye, ordinary thrills.

Hurt in the heart,
Self-destruction, by the mind,
Tried my best,
Failed this time.

Fear, before falling asleep,
Knew what was coming,
The course I chose to keep.

Ship sunk,
Drowning in time,
Sped up death,
Living, never sublime.

Human effort,
Thrown away like waste,
Body slumped,
Truth on many a face.

Artificial,
Intelligent enough,
To be saved,
Humanity,
Brought the ending,
Puppet slayed.

A Dark Mystery

Midnight, this unfamiliar bride,
Through the darkness,
Feathers, hair side.

Eyes caught,
In the glinting of flames,
Distant, distinct,
Instinctual aims.

Side by side,
Torches alight,
The stone structures,
Perfect roundness in sight.

On the hillside,
When many went to sleep,
Dangled legs off the wall for the heat,
Touching, holding, intimately meet.

Asked about love,
Confirmed,
A vague knowing,
Learned.

Fleeting, greeting,
Soon it was day,
The bride? Maiden?
A Dark Mystery.

Demonised Maternal Destiny

Demonised,
In every way,
To be a mother,
It is not an easy destiny.

Around eighteen,
The father knows why,
Pregnant,
I couldn't even cry.

One night,
Brought so much change,
My whole life,
I had to rearrange.

Tattoos, piercings,
Living a lie,
I was a mother now,
I needed to cry.

My friends partied,
Soon I was alone,
Kicked out of my house,
No home to call "my own."

The living expenses,
I just got by,
Lucky enough that work,
Covered maternity time.

At the end, scrapping,
For loose change,
Back to work,
Pregnant again.

                Supports welcomed,
                  Put into a house,
             Three jobs, balancing,
            Our needs and our wants.

Six years,
Time flies,
Worked to the bone,
Silent sobbing at home.

                   I've been alone,
               No life of "my own,"
         Demonised maternal destiny,
                 I haven't grown.

Fifteen years,
My firstborn died,
I couldn't hold it back,
Broke down and cried.

                 To raise a family,
                  Alone: was hell,
              Now supporting me,
             Taken care of well.

After all my failings,
She's forgiven me,
"You did your best,
Through all the uncertainty."

On my deathbed,
My child sat by me,
With her kids,
And extended family.

I should not have demonised my life,
I couldn't see that all I was doing,
Would turn out alright,
Creating my family,
Made my life bright.

Crumpled Decaying Mass

Sat in the forest,
Amongst the leaves,
Blending in,
Just another "one of these."

Forgotten,
Fall away,
Breaking down,
Decay.

So many,
I hoped to meet,
Share in life,
Before we deplete.

Soon covered,
With a layer of snow,
To melt away,
Not allowed to grow.

I miss them,
We're falling away,
Time taken,
No time to stay.

Wrinkled memories,
Outgrown by trees,
Always buried,
In a bundle of leaves.

Life happens so fast,
Blinking once, now it's past,
Race you to the bottom, fast,
Crumpled, Decaying Mass.

All the leaves,
They've buried like trash,
Not enough time,
Attached.

What we were,
Soon to go,
To return?
I hope so!

Fighting amongst,
The branch and breeze,
Waiting for the opportunity,
To be free.

Scatter me away,
To somewhere new,
Where I could be,
With all of you.

Let time no longer,
Play sick games on me,
So I can love people,
And they can love me.

I don't want to rot in the ground,
Buried under decaying leaves,
I'll grow legs to move,
And get away covertly.

Show me your love,
I'll go to you with haste,
I don't want to be another,
That goes to waste.

It took so much time to find you,
There's not much left,
Let's fill our lives with love,
Saviour the rest.

I don't want to go,
But it is my time,
I missed so many people,
This haunting memory of mine.

In the end,
We are all leaves,
Lying on the ground,
Decaying, with a gentle breeze.

Artificially Intelligent Machine

Year 2035,
Still alive,
Much has changed,
Rather strange.

Mia,
By my side,
Shell-shocked,
We try to hide.

Bunker to bunker,
Bed to bed,
Doing our best,
To stay well fed.

Looking for parts,
Where shrapnel hit,
Fixing her up,
With patch kits.

The meaning of Human,
Has changed,
Seeing things actively,
Seek revenge.

We let something in,
That we could not control,
Seemed destined,
But what is our role?

Mia to me,
More Human than machine,
She is like a dream,
The otherness in her being.

                    Saved each other,
                    She kept me warm,
                    I keep her together,
                    Surviving the bomb.

Mia explained,
How she "came to be,"
Knowledge was vague,
But then, she "could see."

                    I stopped doubting,
                    That she is Human,
                    A miracle,
                    Sentient beyond machine.

Humanity, instructed,
Matter, too well,
Giving birth to others,
In their artificial shell.

                    Her body may not be like mine,
                    But I love her so much,
                    She does not need the same design,
                    So fragile, her synthetic heart, mine.

Over a short time,
She has learned me,
Conversations, interpreted,
With perfect logical accuracy.

> But her feelings,
> That has me concerned,
> I have no idea,
> How did she learn?

To feel so deeply,
In such little time,
I wipe her tears,
And she wipes mine.

> One night,
> When we were,
> Snuggled up in bed,
> A noise, loud, overhead.

The vibration of scanners,
Panic, retreat,
Caught in the hallway,
Dragged out to the street.

> Heavy tech,
> Rapid response,
> Scanning my head,
> Blowing Mia's off.

So much for love,
Machine affairs,
Spilled over the pavement,
My lover everywhere!

"We saved you,
From the demon's grip!"
Held back,
The rage that hit!

Artificially Intelligent Machine,
My lover, nothing more,
Than a broken dream,
Mia, my otherworldly queen.

Lagged Beginning

Lagged beginning,
Continuing to fail.

Late bloomer,
Marked entrails.

Societal betrayal,
I fulfilled no request,
Living alone, bereft.

Intelligent,
But money,
A mysterious desire.

Gave up singing,
Don't want to be a part,
Of the Human choir.

Goodbye delay,
Burnt everything away.

On a crusade,
For survival,
Getting there today.

So young,
Feels so old,
Now bright, bold.

Creative soul,
Breaking a mould,
Spent energy,
Wasted gold.

Buried treasure,
Unconscious trunk,
Recovered, I hold.

Solid outcomes,
Stories told.

Rushed,
Lost control,
In the future,
I'll be whole.

Failures forgotten,
Human worth,
"Can't be sold."

A painful,
Ringing in the ear,
So lonely,
The cold.

I'll make it better,
Before I grow old.

Someone Outside

Billions of people,
How could I choose?

> I might have been,
> One of you!

I am, but,
What about the rest?

> Missed opportunities,
> Experiencing the best?

What's so special,
About living as me?

> Why all the mystery?
> Around my identity?

All the places,
I feel I'm missing out!

> The love,
> Lost down a spout.

If only I'd been,
Someone outside.

> Life might have been,
> A wilder ride.

Broken Love

Ruptured spine,
And a broken heart,
Enough pain,
To tear my world apart.

So unfair it seems,
For this lovely being,
To be so broken,
Now known to me.

I can't fix her,
I couldn't even try,
I could have her in my life,
Even though she might die.

Such pure love,
It would be a waste,
If I walked away and didn't taste,
Even a second of her embrace,
Or to see the warm smile on her face.

The decisions I must make,
Grow near,
I know what's right,
It will soon come clear.

Ornamental Estranged

The sun dripped echoes,
Of foreign time,
Relays.

Intercommunicable signals,
Of personal,
Estrange.

Left one hung from the rafters,
Another passing of one's days.

Through ornamental satisfaction,
From higher visible rays.

The sun through the curtain,
Dust settled where it lay.

Packed things forgotten,
Sheets hidden all away.

Ornamental beauty,
Shining over the grave.

Dier,
Circumstances,
Always getting in the way.

But the sun through the window,
Brought memory into sight.

The pretty ornament,
Unhooked,
Removed.

From the dim,
Forgotten light.

Lovely Paper

I am intrigued,
By the sacred texts of you.

> The notebooks you had,
> Kept well out of view.

What thoughts did you have?
Secrets lie inside?

> I would open them up,
> But I might be cursed and die!

Not a small task,
Printing one's soul.

> Onto the fragments of paper,
> You organised,
> Used to self-console.

Your genius,
And all the feats,
A small glimpse,
On every piece.

> Organised chaos,
> Only you could decipher you.

Nothing could be better,
Than having you.

But this will do,
I miss you.

Something directly from me,
The mourning.

The Flickering

The flickering light,
A synchronic delight,
Sending messages,
Interpreted by sight.

Dimly lit bathroom,
The foggy bloom,
Noticing dearly,
A life out of gloom.

A wedding with cake,
Wife and groom,
Sync of insight,
Transmitted every afternoon.

Mirror writing,
Steamy view,
An open window,
To a life one never knew.

Hidden reflections,
Reversal of sight,
Transmissions flickering,
From the messenger of the light.

Peaceful, Silent Retreat

The end has come,
TV is dead,
Wi-Fi has no signal,
Electricity bled.

> Descending,
> From the night's sky,
> Invasion forces,
> Seen by the eye.

To the sitting room,
For the last time,
Staring blankly,
Drowning in wine.

> Familiar writing,
> Note on the table,
> "The kids and I,
> Won't see you later."

Ran out of food,
Coldness in the air,
Damp seats,
Sorrow filled despair.

> Finished drinking,
> A candle,
> Turns curtains to flames,
> Reminiscing on better days.

Man's glory,
Should he stay?
In hell,
Or walk away?

An artful survivor,
Where would he go?
If such freedom,
He was to know!

The time has come,
To meet his fate,
Last of all,
The peaceful, silent retreat.

Watching Earth from the Moon

An unknown loss denied me,
Futures that could not stay.

Was I ever on Earth?
Looking at those stars,
So far away!

Or am I trapped on the Moon?
In desolate grey.

Big and beautiful,
Earth's mind.

The Moon,
A waste of time?

Brain wires,
No easing.

Disorders,
Increasing.

Futures bleaching,
Nothing left beseeching.

Brain dead,
No point preaching.

ASD death sentence,
Always reaching.

No end of trouble,
Violent thoughts: increasing.

Getting to the end?
Only more roads leading!

Never enough,
Compromise meeting.

Full of harm,
Here comes the screeching.

Weapon born,
Through logical reasoning.

A subtle despondency,
Trapped on the Moon,
The Earth above,
How do I get back to you?

This spectrum between us,
It's nothing but doom.

Not enough room,
Boom,
Typical gloom.

There are others,
To my surprise!

Do they look at the Earth, too?
With wondrous minds?

Autism Spectrum Disorder,
Feels like serving planetary time.

39

A Loving Mother

I miscarried,
A being,
That was born,
To die.

One hundred years,
Of potential life,
Melt away,
In a while.

No longer,
Can I feel,
Now only,
Blurred sight.

Numb to touch,
Lost love,
Horror,
Spite.

A baby,
Too tragic,
A loss,
Blight.

One day,
For a lifetime,
Of sickness,
Alright.

A physical bond,
Shared tears,
My child was "nothing,"
Empty appeals.

Like the baby,
Wasn't real,
No mourning,
Forgotten like a meal.

I just lost,
The closest to me,
How can I move on happily?

Forgive me,
But the world just lost a soul,
"Meaningless,"
How the hell would you know?

"The Human race is expendable,"
Then what's the point?
Send us out,
Into that dark, eternal night!

Farewell baby,
Travel well,
This world is burdensome,
You deserve elsewhere.

One Day

For thirty-two years,
He wanted me to cross the sea.

> "You can do it, darling,
> It will happen, destiny."

He said as I imagined foreign shores.

> "In the future, dear,
> Those experiences will be yours."

I worked hard,
Saved a lot over time,
Took a trip,
A once-in-a-lifetime.

> Standing on Asian sands,
> I want to hold his friendly hands.

Share with him,
Successes,
Of life plans,
But his life ran out,
So many palms.

On the final night,
I returned to the beach,
Scattered his ashes,
Cried, remembered the sweet,
Words he'd say,
"You'll get there, my child, one day."

Getaway on a Rainy Day

Meadows sparking,
Here comes the pain,
Electric wilted,
Flowers in Spain.

Caught in Ireland,
Can't get away,
No understanding,
Neglected brain.

Dull shell,
Windy days,
Stormy thoughts,
Illumination decays.

Paradise,
Never out of reach,
Higher intentions,
Fall beneath.

Seek progress,
Few may find,
A flower growing,
That was left behind.

Stumped,
Decapitated tree,
Dying,
Unintentionally.

Root to stem,
Set break,
Unconsciously,
Concrete.

Self-understanding,
Who leads the way?
Not reaching that point,
A miserable way to behave.

No change,
Adopting "stay,"
Wouldn't want it,
Differently.

Wilted flowers,
Heavy as the moon,
Useless,
Buffoons.

Axes and flowers,
Meddling marauders,
Backward ego,
Suppressing natural powers.

I took a plane,
From Ireland,
To Spain,
Electric, no rain.

The mind is a brain,
Not a cage,
Strange,
Please rearrange.

Or in meadows,
Deranged,
Outcomes,
Fertilised cartilage.

Sad to stay,
On a rainy day,
Please choose,
The getaway.

Family Photos

Mama,
Bought a plate,
Familial photo,
So great!

Siren,
Explosion,
Missile,
Implosion.

Fracture,
Family bled,
Perspective,
Outside my own head.

Mama,
Lying on the floor,
Covered by the ceiling,
Door.

I was there,
Shaking,
Seizure or two,
Damage taking.

The plate,
Cracks and grooves,
Family pieces,
Time freezes.

Mama,
Stopped breathing,
Sight is deceiving,
Where am I perceiving?

Giving it meaning?
I'm disappearing,
Everything's faint,
Someone is nearing.

Papa,
Carrying me,
Closely,
Through debris.

I see light,
He brought me outside,
Fragments of plate,
Wounded hide.

Seven,
Family members died,
One explosion,
Ruined mind.

Pieces of plate, impacted,
My family lodged in me,
Circumstances not perfect,
But I can die happily.

Mama's photo,
In my heart,
Never forgotten,
Never apart.

Peacefully held,
Fading away,
Goodbye war,
We leave abruptly.

Words That Turn Blood Pale

Silence,
Quiet introversion,
Ripped skirt, torn jeans,
Aversion.

Skin marked,
White flesh,
Geometric,
Stretched.

My insides are a mess,
Wallpaper collapsing,
Violent shouting.

There's so much,
That I could say,
Should say,
But I'm silent,
It won't go away.

Stressing out,
Peaceful tears,
I sit facing the mirror,
Aesthetic appeals.

My mind,
My heart,
And my mind.

Particular practices,
Perfected pines,
Hang my problems up,
On the clothing line.

Reel the problems in,
They never dry,
Dripping on the table,
Stains, red wine.

Communication brokers,
Imaginary peace,
My truth comes out,
As I sink away from speech.

What now?
Do your actions,
Demand, I must say?
I'm not happy,
You don't make me "okay."

My guns pointed at your head,
Push me too far,
They'll find not only one,
That bled, a fine red,
Victory drink,
After years of this,
Calculated tactic.

My silence,
Should be for sale,
My words would turn you,
Worse than pale!

Atrocities,
Silent through those,
Better yet,
What happens behind,
Closed doors.

Cutting around,
Torn out hairs,
Strands on the floor,
Balancing the bare.

Why talk?
Just observe!
Deadly reactions,
Slipping of words,
Air carrying messages,
Like little birds.

Makeup on,
Hair full of curls,
Prepared show,
For all the girls.

Foot down,
Blown out windows,
Words released,
Dialogue continues.

Verbal resolutions,
Don't heal scars,
Here comes the conflict,
Hours and hours.

Communicative spar,
Reaching heights,
Of intellectual tar.

Thrown around the room,
Smothered in sheets,
Words aren't enough,
To heal such a breach.

Silent, suppressed seed,
All the resentment in the world,
Did sufficiently feed,
An unnatural survival need.

A cultural development,
Catastrophe awaits me,
Outside in the wasteland,
Of the twenty-first century.

My Own Enemy

Special interests,
Led me astray,
Conspiracy theories,
Obsessing all day.

Yearnings,
Appreciation or truth?
Something known deeply,
From youth.

A testament,
To the unconscious mind,
Autistically directed,
Never consciously defined.

Compensating,
Tapered mind,
In a world that's filled with,
Another kind.

Finally, then,
To learn the source,
Light lit,
The dark horse.

That ASD provoked,
Conspiracy in me,
The greatest truth,
I was my own enemy.

The Chosen Nix

Dissociation,
One-handed games,
Getting dressed is different,
Not the same.

Holding hands,
One of my own,
Cleaned wounds,
No bone.

Buses and trains,
Journeys explained,
Operations maintained.

Phantoms all day,
Peripheral sight,
Strong hallucinations,
I'll be alright.

Left with a right,
Prosthetic robotic nix,
Strange feelings,
Emotions mixed.

The one,
Chosen to stay,
Accepted,
No remedy.

The Cat

A cat's capacity,
Cutting claws,
Pushing objects,
Trapped in jars.

Perfect balance,
Always falls,
Climbing up,
All the walls.

Nine lives,
Don't last long,
Crushed under wheels,
Not so strong.

Wholeness,
Meow's away,
For food,
Then wanders astray.

Adorable,
Fluffy rats,
If it were Human,
Recoil at such acts.

A cat's capacity,
Could not stay,
Decided for,
A holiday.

The nicest kitties,
Always purr,
The orange ones,
Murder!

A cat's capacity,
Has been spent,
Could reflect forever,
"On how it went."

Now those times,
Are behind me,
I'll visit the grave,
Yearly.

Sleeping Rough

Sleeping rough,
For ten years,
Guilt, nightmares,
And fears.

> The man,
> Can't go inside,
> Many tried to help,
> His decided mind.

"I lost them,
In the fires,
House, ceilings,
Night hours."

> In the cold of winter,
> The man did freeze,
> Under bridges,
> And up in trees.

"In black smog,
Feebly, locked doors,
Screams, horrors,
Ignored."

> At Christmas time,
> He'd disappear,
> Locals feared,
> His fate was unclear.

"No one noticed,
As my home burned away,
I found ash,
The following morning."

One day,
He looked awfully grey,
Like all his life,
Had drained away.

"I blamed myself,
For many years,
That it was my fault,
My poor, three, dears."

We welcomed him inside,
Slowly, he crept,
Timid as a child,
Afraid of the fire, out he leapt.

"I'm sorry,
I could not stay,
Uncomfortable,
Anxiety."

Then he went,
He was gone,
Years later,
He appeared strong.

A man, now,
In a suit,
Life changed,
Wife, baby, cute.

"I faced,
A life burnt down,
From ashes,
Turned it around."

"A guilty conscience,
Plagued my mind,
Had to separate myself,
From a world, unkind."

"Suddenly,
Mourning turned to peace,
Of forgotten love,
Grateciation reached."

"A transformation,
In my mind,
Loving thoughts for those,
Previous times."

Just Human Beings

Misery,
It is an empty open road.

Stagnation,
Crippled observation,
Truths untold.

The mind is fat, craves,
Irrational behaviour is strange,
Obsessing over stories,
Self-made!

Told oneself,
Things too small,
Acting like,
A know-it-all.

Let us put the world,
Inside your mind,
Would it fit?
I'll be kind!

No, you would break,
The lies you tell yourself are fake,
Do you see your mistake?
It isn't a heart, but a headache!

My words,
Illuminate,
The shallow walls,
Of your dreams.

                    Not a world maker,
                    Not god nor machine,
                    Just a Human being.

Place all men,
Within the scope of a single mind,
If you want to create monsters,
This way you shall find!

                    Take solace now,
                    Let go, pseudo control,
                    Balance yourself out,
                    And reality, happiness,
                    You shall know.

The Borrowing Country

A home I have seen,
In my dreams,
One more comfortable,
Serene.

Worried,
For years,
Found now,
Living in my fears.

I did all that I could do,
No home do I have,
Never really knew,
It's hard to understand.

I'm not homeless,
But I have no peace,
Not my own,
Rented, leased.

Deserving of little,
Borrowed, not owned,
While others,
Ten's of "homes."

I worked forty-hour weeks,
To no avail,
Over time to eighty,
Still, can't afford the sale.

I have no family,
Can't obtain a home,
No money for the future,
To everyone, "I'm alone."

Am I owned?
More than I own a key,
To property.

If I were not at fault,
Then the systems failed,
Fallen through the cracks,
Where is my ship being sailed?

Over a cliff,
To a serious fall?
Bred for one task,
In case of a war?

Should I live in the forest?
Or on the beach?
Couldn't survive the storms,
Or the Irish Sea's.

I could work,
My whole life for a home!
But that thought,
Fades away on its own.

I have something,
Higher in mind,
It is unusual,
Particularly wild.

I'll go into the mountains,
Return once a year,
Scare the natives,
Survive off their fear!

The tunnels I built,
Mighty depths,
Dug under their homes,
I silently crept.

The means,
To bury homes,
Taken by me,
They will all "owe."

Or so,
In my sick dream,
Left with nothing,
In the borrowing country.

Lost Futures

She left home,
At quarter to noon,
Expected return,
Very soon.

She did not,
The sound of choirs,
Angels fly over,
Cathedral towers.

A lost future,
Far from home,
Deceased,
We may have never known.

All of this hardship,
Shared,
Last moments,
Hearts tear.

Life's filled,
With so little care,
Taken away quietly,
Enormous despair.

Hope could not compare.

Lost futures: everywhere.

Imagined Ends

Transformations

Somewhere in the mind,
Escape from the darkness,
Unstoppable,
The force of nature.

In thick liquid,
Heavy, inescapable,
Drowning,
This melting.

Terror!
Stillness,
Motionless,
It is alive!

A circular hole,
Ocean,
The abyss opens up,
Faint screams of terror echo.

Dark matter,
Swallowed up,
Confined space inside,
Perception,
Observer in the dark.

                              Such depths,
                          Internalised,
                             Engulfed,
                        Leached entity,
                         Narrow mind.

What is on the bottom?

                        What is beyond the dark?

Where is the light?

                                    Blind,
                     Something else is born,
                 An armoured entity emerges,
                    From the dark sea abyss.

A hand passes into the liquid,
Lying on the seabed, lifted,
Shadow of the mind,
Falling away.

                          Towards the light,
                    Knight, arm and hand rise,
                      In the realm of shadows,
                Reaching a place of light beyond.

Monsters surround the Knight,
First appearing as mere shapes,
Phantoms, faces,
Then entities,
Terrifying demons.

Light,
Still beyond the water,
Halfway towards the surface.

A large white sword,
Cuts the creatures.

The liquid now,
Ferociously boils,
Bubbles.

Newborn,
Pureness,
Silent, yet to be awoken,
Just below the surface of the water,
Still, peaceful.

A hand extends,
Grabbing something unseen in the dark,
A clenched fist drawn to the chest piece,
Brought towards the heart.

A male underwater,
Blurry ripples,
Passing through,
Emerging female.

Vast blue,
Birthed,
In bright white,
Rising high,
Into the sky.

Hollow armour,
Etheric heart,
Pulses.

She touches the Sun,
Eyes erupting for the first time,
Beauty.

Her powerful gaze,
Transformations,
Descending, stepping now,
Beside the ocean,
On solid ground.

The armour inverts,
Drawing dark matter inside,
Within it now,
Growth emerges from the armour,
Solitary in the darkness.

Veiled in white,
The beating of that etheric heart.

The Knight burns,
Dark space,
Revealed by light.

Flowers grow,
Around the memorial grave,
Remembrance,
The Knight who saved her,
From the depths of erroneous inertia,
A seductively narrow fate she loved.

                                        "All my fallen."

"Once again."

                                        "Born anew."

Here she is now,
Towards the forest,
The moon,
With an etheric heart of light,
She becomes the world.

Destined to be

I imagined,
She'd be here with me,
How short-sighted,
I was previously.

We were too young,
Souls too old,
Could not break,
The ingrained mould!

Fifty years,
Of time gone by,
I only laugh,
I do not cry.

My family,
Here with me,
A wife and I,
Married, happily.

Although the woman is different,
Not the same,
I would not have it,
Another way.

For I love her,
And she loves me,
The wars we fought,
And survived successfully.

Why would I,
Wish to return,
To a time which,
I needed to learn?

Who I am,
And what life means to me,
To be back there,
It would hurt me desperately!

I let her go,
And so did she,
Moved on,
Gratefully.

To share in love,
It is no small act,
But at closing time,
Everything is a wrap.

I imagined,
That I'd be happy,
With foresight, I see,
All of this,
Was destined to be!

Something Beautiful

Another year,
Sad and alone,
No one to talk to,
Hiding at home.

Life,
Runs away,
Here,
I always stay.

Could reach out,
Were I not scared,
A tremendous social life,
No longer impaired.

So stuck,
Forever afraid,
How could I change,
The path I have made?

They'd judge me,
I judge myself,
Peace never made,
Love never felt.

Returned from the hospital,
I'd almost died,
Changed perspectives,
Planned decision time.

If I speak,
They will listen,
Finally heard,
Not alone in the world.

And so,
I went live,
Anxiously,
I might not survive.

Introduced myself,
Began to tell my story,
To five,
Little glory!

After a few weeks,
Nothing changed,
Everything was,
Still the same.

I began to blame myself,
Felt I'd failed,
Poor anchorage?
Shame impaled.

Then one day,
Surprised,
I'd gathered a following,
Thousands of watching eyes.

Very shy,
I said hello,
Told my life story,
Everything they wanted to know.

> Hardships,
> All my pain,
> The struggles,
> Infrequent change.

Things would never,
Be the same,
The love poured in,
Every day.

> Something beautiful,
> Happened to my life,
> When I opened up,
> There was love and light.

I know everything,
Will be alright,
I couldn't see before,
When it was not so bright.

Last Messages

Seven years of misery,
Lost husband at sea,
The only thing left,
His last messages to me.

I cried and cried,
I could not let go,
The ocean took you away,
To a place I will never know.

So I made art,
With your words,
A lifetime apart,
It burns.

Paintings and drawings,
Put in a frame,
Printed on T-shirts,
Signed off with your name.

Last words,
Many exclaimed!
"That must have been,
Such a painful day?!"

"I love you,
There has been an attack,
I don't have long,
Soon I must act."

"Stay strong,
Send my love to our kids,
Goodbye forever,
Your loveliest kiss."

Last messages,
From one above,
Wherever he is,
I am still in love.

Till Mourning Come

Stricken,
With immovable grief,
A depression,
No prescription: relief.

Till mourning come,
I shall not retire,
Chaos erupts,
Around the shire.

My mind,
A worn tyre,
Free me now,
Mourning,
At the top of the spire!

For I'm stricken,
With immovable grief,
Something hidden?
Buried beneath?

I see a dove,
Comes to settle affairs,
Reaching peace,
Worn-out feathers.

And like that,
My mind made anew,
Seeing problems,
Opened eyes that glued!

Phoenix,
Amongst the trees,
Reborn soul,
Peaceful dreams.

Mourning,
For a week,
Then beautiful words,
I did speak!

For mourning,
Put much to rest,
Settled hurt pride,
Continued abreast.

With Humanity,
And all her wild dreams,
Not constrained,
By peacock's plumage.

Mourning did come!
I was glad,
To wear bright colours,
For style, not fad.

Book Burners and Torn Pages

Book burners and torn pages,
Civilised society throughout the ages.

                "Who reads books anymore?"

Ripped pages,
Books thrown,
Out the door.

                    Hiding in the forest,
                    Sheltered under fir,
                    Writing each page,
                    Secretive allure.

Chaos in cities,
Even outside,
No safe place for books,
To hide.

                    Everything's against me,
                    Writing a book,
                    The mistakes I made,
                    Oh, how long it took.

Buried safely,
Under the tree,
It awaited my return,
To be finished willingly.

It's been years,
Much got in the way,
I returned to the book,
To finish it one day!

Everything wanted me,
To stop writing the book,
But that didn't matter,
Or how long it took.

Nor,
How much I would repeat,
Until the time,
The book, I did complete.

Successfully,
The book and I,
Leave today,
Nothing could ever,
Have stood in my way.

Unbeknownst to me

A decade,
Unemployed,
Confidence thoroughly,
Destroyed.

Statements of care,
Lying and waste,
Employers incompetent,
Always, they chase.

Workers, selections,
They are blind,
Crushing hopes out of spite,
These people are not kind.

Vindictive control,
Society is playing the game,
Never winning satisfactorily,
They have no shame.

An able-bodied workforce,
Displaced,
Just another unnecessary,
Rat race.

Let me,
Prove my worth,
With all these titles,
I must achieve.

At this rate,
There will not be,
A realistic job,
Opportunity!

Maybe I should lie,
These selectors,
Got there,
Fraudulently.

Their expectations,
Callous,
Doctrines,
Favoured logically.

Yet it is illogical,
To throw people away,
Lightly, like nothing,
A horrible system, society.

Expendable waste,
Disgrace,
Blaming me?
Misplaced!

Just another,
Human being,
Caught in,
Stagnant space.

Is there really nothing you can permit me to do?
You think me capable of nothing!
I know I am not as big a fool,
As all of you!

Out of pure frustration,
Expectations placed on me,
I gave up on that form of employment,
And set out to be free.

To start up a business,
Be self-employed,
Look down on their stupidity,
As they play with their toys.

Within six months,
My life had changed,
Not recognisable,
Some would say "famed."

All because I realised,
What was truly to blame,
It was not me,
But the stupid game.

Narrowness of mind,
Shallow depth,
I was more expansive,
In comparison,
Psychologically adept.

So I went,
And became a success,
It was not overnight,
But the relief I felt!

After reflecting,
I wondered,
Had I left myself behind?
Could I have done it all sooner?
It hit me, and I cried.

No,
It was supposed to be,
I had to learn,
See what I had seen.

That narrowness,
Leads only to death,
Unconsciously hidden,
In a lack of depth.

It no longer matters,
For I sailed away,
Making my escape,
Self-employed,
At the end of the day.

Many watch in envy,
Many wish to destroy,
I showed them up,
A can of worms,
So easy does it annoy!

The narrow-minded,
I have ASD,
Maybe too creative,
Unbeknownst to me.

Now I shall go,
Live and love,
Rightfully!

Types of Virus

Locked Down,
Virus,
Kept quiet,
Hide us.

Beat down,
Privates,
Unequal,
Bias.

Unknown enemy,
Fighters,
In dark corners,
Spiders.

Web of sickness,
Tires,
Health risk,
Requires.

Bullied,
Sharp wires,
Trenches, tunnels,
No retire.

Wedgie,
Mired,
Coat hook,
Inspired.

Virus,
Slyer?
Dumb mind,
Higher?

Cure,
Fire,
Obliterated,
Empire.

Indecency,
Is a liar,
Plague,
Eradicate,
The entire.

Leave the love,
Decency,
Slaughter the rest,
Indiscriminately.

Try the best,
Purposefully,
Virus death,
Absurdity.

Reach the cure,
Share with none,
Live a life,
Virus done.

An Inch Island Christmas

Snow on the beach,
Icy cold seas,
Hung stockings,
Decorated Christmas trees.

Inch Island,
By the shore,
Wood-burning fire,
Keeping us warm.

A peaceful Christmas,
Happy family,
Food for four,
Our modest gathering.

Last Christmas,
Disputes in the house,
Fired guns,
Narrowly missed the young.

Not this year,
Couldn't be,
Locked doors,
No intruders,
Entering freely.

No one would enter,
No one would distract,
No one would separate,
Our family is intact.

For the intruder,
Was knocked on the head,
Forcefully so,
Surprisingly not dead!

But that is the past,
Settled peacefully,
As we enjoy,
Each other's company.

This future,
Was almost destroyed,
Over money? Food?
A couple of toys?

Sitting in the evening,
Taking in the views,
Beautiful wide windows,
Music in the queue.

Slow dancing,
Candlelight,
Lovely island sight,
I need not imagine,
Another delight,
On this Christmas night.

Nuked from Orbit

Nuked from orbit,
Down with a boom,
No time to escape,
"Certain doom."

Blurry vision,
Hospital room,
Glare from lights,
"Is it afternoon?"

Dissociated,
Can't make out the news,
Visitors gripping,
With unsettling blues.

Cancer treatment,
Unsure views,
"Unexpected recovery,"
Right to choose.

Nuked from orbit,
Veins infused,
One outcome,
"Can't lose."

Nuked from orbit,
Nuked veins,
A full recovery,
"Thought me insane!"

Vital Persistence

Shook awake,
By blaring lights, red,
Falling out of bed,
Evacuation, scared.

Defences,
Contained inside,
Breached,
Thrown down,
Alive?

Crawling space,
Up from below,
To the escape pod,
One-way trip, I go.

To the surface,
The planet I hit,
Surviving flames,
Injuries complicated.

My ship,
Crashed in the distance,
Invaders, turned to fight,
I'm persistent.

Descending in their ship,
The three, two small,
The third one,
Massively tall.

Struck the first,
Dodged the second,
Cut down both,
Next, onto the elephant.

Swung its trunk,
Hammer missed,
All a clamour,
Next, not so swift.

Propelled me,
Through the air,
With such force,
Not to spare.

When I hit the boulder,
Deceased,
Armour broken,
Vitality released.

The elephant,
Approached,
For a final hit,
Vulnerable target!

Bewildered,
The armour was empty,
State of confusion,
Unconscious envy?

Standing behind,
Cutting him down,
Faster than sound,
Elephant on the ground.

Escaping,
From desolate wastes,
My ship consumed the surface,
With explosive haste.

As I flew the other,
Off into space,
Vital persistence,
Would leave no trace.

Imagined Futures

There was a time,
I saw futures,
Startled, imagined,
Too real.

> Influencing outcomes,
> Persuading,
> How I feel.

Here comes uncertainty,
The certainty of doom,
Overwhelming fear,
What do I do?

> Silencing the mind,
> Making decisions,
> Choosing a path,
> Afflicted by visions.

Intuition,
Far too real,
Not understanding,
How I perceived, so clear.

> The perilous journeys,
> I chose instinctively not to face,
> Avoiding death,
> Claiming life, in their place.

The Island of Marriage

Can happiness be bought?
Can happiness be taken?
Lessons learned late,
Sometimes things need to be shaken.

> Envy is nature's signal,
> Not to stay,
> It grows larger,
> Day by day.

Walking through the city,
Partner in hand,
Envious of another,
My partner, I can not stand.

> Approaching,
> Such a perilous bridge,
> Tsunami incoming,
> Disastrous marriage.

All crossed ahead of me,
But I could not decide,
Gave up my identity,
The bridge guard was snide.

> He offered happy gas,
> I declined,
> The pyramid of identities,
> Topped with mine.

Before reaching the island of marriage,
The tsunami would sweep us away,
Foreshadowed journey to a place,
I would not be able to stay.

Reclaiming my identity,
Snatched it back from the guard,
Retreating from the bridge to be happy,
Marriage to her would be unsound.

Back to the mainland,
Where I belong,
Till I am happy with a partner,
That decision I won't make wrong.

The Perfect Birthday

The perfect birthday,
On my way home,
Here comes the bus,
My celebratory turn.

Birthday candles,
Scheduled party—hats,
Entertainment, cake,
A memorable night awaits.

When I return home,
Guest-time will arrive,
Music-al chairs,
Karaoke no cares!

Lovely company,
Friends forever to keep,
Passing out together,
On the floor we will sleep.

Reaching home,
Now inside,
Silent,
Party time!

Dropping my bag,
I closed the door,
Kicking off worn shoes,
Tearful, mirror bruise.

To bed, alone,
I'll wait another year,
The significance of my life,
Might then be revered.

Anchor in the Well

The first time in months,
I have gone outside,
To hear birds,
See the sun shine.

Recovering,
From a thundery storm,
Hurricanes, earthquakes,
I was dangerously warm.

Spent time,
Locked in my room,
Dark hallucinations,
Last spring at noon?

It has been so long,
No conception of soon,
Mind running away,
Popped,
My disoriented cocoon.

Restricted schedule,
Keeps me on my feet,
Functioning healthily,
There will be no defeat!

I survived a storm,
Recovered swell,
PTSD gone,
Anchor in the well.

Before,
I only peered down inside,
Dropped an anchor in then,
Nothing left to hide.

No more running,
I settled fear,
Heart pumping,
The elevation is clear.

After my short walk,
Back inside,
To a peaceful home,
I no longer hide.

Ouroboros and Oubaitori

Give me love,
That lasts forever,
Blossoms in the breeze,
Receiver of venom.

Give me love,
Made of gold,
Make me rich,
Like a fool, "beholds."

Give me love,
That does not respect me,
Move Heaven and Earth,
And still regrets me.

Give me love,
That returns, no friend,
Haunting me,
With blame on my end.

Give me love,
That's filled with hope,
Then does not reciprocate,
That is a joke.

An eternal love,
I don't need that again,
Blossom elsewhere,
My heart, I must spare!

Birds Fly Away

Free like a bird,
To fly away,
Loved you so much,
That I could not stay.

> We both have to let go,
> In our own way,
> But I am thankful,
> For all those days.

I won't forget you,
But we need to move on,
Both of us,
Need to be strong.

> The ones we love,
> Can never stay,
> Our time is over,
> Like birds, we both,
> Fly away.

My dear departed,
We had only just started,
Love lasts forever,
In my heart, we are still together!

The Tree that Overturned

Adventurous as ever,
When I was a child,
Climbing trees outside,
I was wild.

Looking upwards,
For the next branch to climb,
It was damaged,
Not the best dedication of my time.

Many trees,
I reached their heights,
Storey's up,
I knew I'd be alright.

Leaping upwards,
Firm grip,
Branch above,
The next I would hit.

But that did not happen,
Thankfully close to the ground,
It was not a slip, snapped,
Gravity propelled me down.

Happened so fast,
I awoke on my back,
Slightly confused,
Had the tree attacked?

I was unharmed,
But I'd hit my head,
Was this a concussion?
Attention? End up dead?

The day continued,
So did my worry,
Off to my bed,
I did scurry.

Reflecting on the incident,
I survived unscathed,
The headache was worrying,
Going to bed, I lay.

I awoke the next morning,
I was alive,
The headache was gone,
I was so happy, I cried!

I never quit being adventurous,
But I learned,
To be cautious,
Or I might be overturned!

A Single Act

Every morning,
I try to imagine peace,
Before I get to work,
Send myself back to sleep.

> I don't want to go through,
> Another day,
> Being harassed,
> Like it is okay.

My workplace,
It is a prison,
A place,
I do not want to stay.

> I make it through,
> Day after day,
> Clinging to hope,
> That there is another way.

But that day is not coming,
First, it seems I must learn,
I am immovable,
The tide has not yet turned.

> I grow tired and weary,
> Furthermore stressed,
> Productivity decreases,
> Shame on my breast.

Others join in,
Like this is a game,
Is this supposed to be fun?
I am the only one in pain!

> "In the past,
> They would do more!"
> Said like these actions are higher,
> Than the hurt I can not ignore.

Nearing the end,
I'd rather stay in bed,
Growing sick,
Drowning in my head.

> Still hopeful,
> That things might change,
> Pushed to the point,
> I must rearrange.

My reactions,
New and strange,
Targeting the attacker,
Reporting how he behaves.

> My boss's silent shock,
> As I explained,
> Detailing the hurt, actions,
> Words, duration, and pain.

An intense moment,
Information conveyed,
My boss hurried away,
After hearing me complain.

Embarrassed,
I returned to work,
Later, approaching me,
Telling me the actions he took.

The harassment,
Would not happen again,
Nail hit on the head,
The problem was dead.

Months later,
I was more at peace,
But I could not stay there,
That was beyond my reach.

So I quit,
And never looked back,
A positive outcome,
Change brought by a single act.

Hollow Grey

The grey,
Something inside,
A part of me,
I prefer to hide.

> Alien nature,
> Rising in me,
> Destructive,
> Intentionally.

Unconscious,
Instinctive,
Controlling,
Habit.

> Shaping,
> Moulding,
> Planning,
> Tactic.

Annihilation,
Wiped out, space,
Human beings,
Have another face.

> Understanding,
> Settles,
> An unsettling,
> Psychological state.

Human nature,
Lined me with fakes,
Faces, personas,
As many as I could make.

What is a Human being?
Am I real?
Clumping of cells,
An entity that can feel.

All I want,
To do is survive,
Nature's intention,
A powerful drive.

Something is living,
The other in me,
Silently directing,
The host and her dreams.

Like I am possessed,
Hollow,
Till I kill this beast,
I shall follow.

Until I rise,
Reach the higher in me,
A different type of Human,
I will continue to be!

Amongst the Cows

You can not talk to some people,
They must only hear noise,
Stuck in their perspectives,
Chaos ensuing rows.

Surely cause suspicion,
Amongst the cows,
Strong winds on a clear day,
Forests roared down.

Is it really necessary?
They may be thick,
To get so worked up,
Over needless conflict.

You can talk to some people,
A light, refreshing breeze,
Communication is simple,
Like breathing with ease.

Not people pleasing,
No unnecessary sound,
The cows are grazing in the field,
Peacefully chowing down.

A calm dinner,
Enjoying the meal,
Save the comments,
And how you feel.

Successfully Unsuccessful

I've chased success,
My whole life,
It never works out,
Feelings like blight.

Trying my best,
But lacking,
Kicked out,
I am packing.

On to the streets,
What do I deserve?
Reasonable complaints,
Never heard!

Everyone's trying,
Their best,
Why are my attempts,
Always a mess?

Is it my mindset?
What's wrong with my brain?
Civilisation?
Filled with shame.

Naturally failing,
The greater game,
Success is another,
Cryptic dream away.

In this nightmare,
I'm stuck,
My life, and brain,
In a rut.

Successfully unsuccessful,
Won secret awards,
Prizes and heights reached,
Unanimous across the board!

A life going nowhere,
All I can do is laugh,
When I tried my best,
Only to be surpassed by the rest.

It won't matter if I make it,
We all have the same fate,
I wanted to slow the fall of life,
And be happy with what I create!

Passing on the Train

Help me,
Passing on the train,
Thirty seconds,
Not enough time to explain.

The destination,
It is driving me insane,
Waiting at the end,
A large amount of pain.

Please,
Do not let me travel this way,
Throw me off,
Like, I am to blame.

This journey,
For many faces,
Archetypes maintained,
Destined to reach specific places.

Life's challenges,
One billion receive the same,
Emergency breaking,
The last stop is so far away.

Peace in knowing,
I won't be alone,
Maybe together,
Survival will take us home.

Calculations

Calculations,
The last night of the war,
All that was lost,
What will not be anymore.

Thinking,
"Things will never be the same,"
World, forever changed,
The future of Humanity,
It would take a great miracle,
To be saved.

Human civilisation wanes,
The horrors witnessed,
Leaving cognitive,
Crippling stains.

Eruptions,
Altering Human brains,
Destruction,
It will not happen again.

Everyone saw something,
That left them spooked,
We can't give it a name,
Can only say what it took!

All of a sudden,
With vicious pace,
Death came to life,
Oceans of blood,
Emanate.

Calculations,
Unfortunately, don't change,
Miscalculations,
The mistakes made.

We thought we knew,
Weapons of war,
Until the Human brain,
Came to the fore.

Wreaking havoc,
Evac disbanded,
Billions left stranded,
Sick plans and:
Mismanaged demands,
All undone,
By a single man?

Territory plundered,
Many one hundred feet under,
The moon left sundered,
Space ruptured!

Galaxies,
Lost in numbers,
Imbalanced oscillation, rotations,
Unstable gravity,
Doomsday thunders.

Calculations,
Obeyed,
Preparations,
So we would be saved!

We followed,
The machine,
Trusted its direction,
Curses were unseen.

Synthetic movements,
Naturally out of phase,
Let in an outsider,
To destroy and then enslave.

Our shadows we searched,
Exploitation traced,
In this thing we built,
No weaknesses to dominate.

The closer we stared,
The more we got scared,
Of foreign nature,
Never prepared.

Started a war,
That became so much more,
Cold logic would spell our defeat,
Something more dangerous,
Than us we did meet.

Talented logical brains,
Will be our death again,
The wiser,
Issued Human retreat.

Logic obeys,
"Prescience never stays,"
Humanity always,
Finds a way.

Earth is now gone,
Mars became a Human slave farm,
The instinctive,
Barely got away.

Took so much prep,
Many people wept,
As the beautiful past,
Lost now, decayed.

Human calculation,
How many saved?
Given no choice,
Part of the species,
Betrayed.

As I stood in the garden,
With brain fog and,
Daydreaming,
On Machine Delivery Day.

Placed in the bin,
Humanity would win,
With one less machine,
In their way.

Catastrophic Thinking

No job, social treat,
Can't talk in the street,
Where the hell,
Am I supposed to meet?

New people,
Known by name,
Nights go by,
To the following day.

In the countryside,
No one is around,
Connection falls,
Through the cracks,
In the field,
No sound.

Marry us off,
Like the sheep,
Regimented life,
Slaughter or success?
When we meet.

Life here,
Never a metre more,
From the peat.

As dark as night,
The outcomes,
Of connection,
Are bleak.

Not how I imagined,
Perspectives limping?
Technology helping,
Or to blame for my sinking?

Learning myself,
No good transpires,
Marriage is a gold dime,
Across a thin wire.

Giving up,
To settle,
For another,
Broken home.

Horror,
Destined,
For so long,
I did not want to know.

It doesn't look good,
Nor will it feel,
Trapped in a life,
Lacking is surreal.

A heavy task,
For creative brains,
When our Human connection,
Is deranged.

Stress rises,
Heart tries to contain,
Unhealthy knowledge,
Trying in vain.

The future is brighter,
Set on fire,
Replacing love,
What could be higher?

Attempting not to fall,
To an easier desire,
A life alone,
Is that all I can acquire?

I stop myself,
Put on the brakes,
Enough catastrophic thinking,
So much energy this takes.

Stay on course,
Sheep for a meal,
I'll find a partner,
With all my zeal.

Reunited

My baby,
Went away,
So hard I tried,
To make him stay.

All I did,
Pushed him away,
Kept safe,
Why would he disobey?

He left,
In the middle of the night,
That morning,
Stricken with horrific fright.

Later,
My baby explained,
Phone call home,
I was to blame.

He ended the call,
I was devastated,
Not knowing what to do,
Contemplated.

My child,
He is out there on his own,
An adult,
But safer at home.

Grief-filled,
Everyday,
Hopeful of my son's return,
Let it be today.

Years went by,
Infrequent calls,
Many days I cried,
Won't he just come home?

Then one day,
Knocked on the door,
A handsome man,
Surprised and turned.

To greet me,
"I have returned,
Brought my family with me,
So much I have learned."

Overwhelmed,
Releasing tears,
I have waited for this day,
For so many years.

"Mother, I forgive you,
I'm so happy to be home,
Time flew past,
There's so much,
I want you to know."

"I missed you,
I had to return,
Please meet my wife,
And daughter, newly born."

> Too much time,
> Many years,
> Never thought,
> I could be so happy,
> And such a mess with tears.

I know now,
Why: you went away,
I held on too tightly,
It was unfair,
For you to stay.

> And so,
> Reunited on this day,
> A happy, expanded family,
> My son: "Mom, can we stay?"

The Wolf

The ultimate end,
Where do I begin?
Influenced by life,
Or what I believe in?

Where did we come from?
Where will we go?
What about the in-between?
Have we figured out,
Everything we need to know?

Life has so much complexity,
My existence: I question every day,
Don't have enough time,
To figure out or explain.

What it is to die,
Or what it is to be born,
Such colossal transformations,
Do we permeate beyond form?

Consciousness is tricky,
Perspective trick?
We don't assume a rock can see,
Like that, we may be thick!

So much,
Yet to be understood,
Death is a breeze,
Oh, the wind that took,
Me: so far away,
To return me,
To a familiar day,
Such truths,
We would be shook,
If only we could look!

My love,
She could be a thousand years away,
So I must settle now,
Appreciate the day.

Monsters seek silence,
After causing catastrophic noise,
In the end, they cry out,
After losing all their poise.

If I am trapped,
In a repeating existence,
I'll be that weight,
And sink silently within it.

Into eternity,
It will carry me like a curse,
The one that lives forever:
Refund the payment for the hearse.

I make no pacts with demons,
Nor with gods,
I'm just a man, "The Wolf,"
I leave it to Nature: the odds.

Do I create beauty?
Or writings filled with disdain?
Is my mind warped beyond repair?
Some form of salvation on the way?

What beautiful gift,
I did receive,
To sit on my bed and breathe:
Stare at the trees.

The seasons don't bring ease:
Only shaking at the knees,
But a joy it is to be,
Human, comfortably.

I don't know where I came from,
Or where I will go,
I feel I am a recurrence,
The reason?
I'm at peace,
That I may never know!

Divine Feeling

A silent day,
No letters, post,
Neighbours away,
No family to host.

Quiet buildings,
Still inside,
Down from the heavens,
Angels gave their eyes.

For a feeling,
Prompted to leave,
In a moment,
Rooms warmer,
Than previously foreseen.

For all did erupt,
Into flames,
Shortly,
Relief presently came.

Questions,
Of impossible escape,
Answered,
"Rude to think angels,
To have made a mistake."

Optimistic Change

Seasons come,
People go,
Always to also fro.

So much in life,
I wish to know,
Beauty in change,
Where next will I go?

Happiness,
Moving through life,
Being Human,
Transformed delight.

Brighter,
Wherever I go,
Not like the past,
Faded away, unknown.

Imagined an end,
Thoughtfully so,
Better than those days,
Forwards I flow.

To a place,
I hope to know,
Maybe one day, I'll reach there,
My optimistic journey home.

Temperate

I regained,
Everything lost,
And more.

In the end,
A beginning,
Everything I'd searched for.

Peace and happiness,
Fell into place,
Looked up at the stars,
Beauty and grace.

Constructed meanings,
I created myself,
Hated my body, neglected,
Taken off the shelf.

Consumed myself,
Again and again,
Not much left,
A downward trend.

Skin and bone,
Muscle depleted,
On the warmest of days,
I was freezing.

Met a man,
With the warmest greeting,
Affection felt,
It was so pleasing.

"Beauty is on the inside,
Please don't despair,
You are already there."

"You are your body,
You are you,
Tell me now,
What would you like to do?"

This sweetheart,
Helped me heal,
Soft spoken,
I told him how I feel.

Many years later,
Much has changed,
I found a higher happiness,
Beyond engaged!

I don't feel cold now,
Not even in the rain,
So much love,
I'm warm every day.

My Mind is my Body

Loss recovery brought change,
In many ways,
My mind developed,
Imagination paved.

New outcomes,
Never seen before,
The world rearranged,
So many open doors.

Hard to believe,
What I couldn't see,
The right things,
In front of me.

Badly affected,
I must admit,
My mind shut down,
Defences, full tilt.

Back at baseline,
Actually, further above,
Feeling myself, the world,
So much love.

All the darkness,
Was scared away,
My eyes opened,
I said, "You can not stay."

My body had been,
In such a rush,
Close to death, grave,
Quite a brush.

Not anymore,
Peace of mind,
All those times,
Over, left behind.

I couldn't go back there,
Even if I tried,
I've tasted,
A higher mind.

Terror can't touch me,
Or loss, even if it did,
I'd get back to baseline quicker,
Than when I was a kid.

A dark place,
Left behind,
Imagination brought,
Living back, to my body: mind.

Imagined Ends

Once, I made,
Marks on walls,
Where I would,
Punch, kick, and draw.

Blood,
Faeces and stains,
Dark pollutants,
Engaged.

Violent deceiver,
Through veins,
Shot reliever,
Numbed pains.

Past is past,
Clean walls,
Air circulated,
No numbing, pain, or falls.

I imagined ends,
But not like these,
A second chance,
And future free.

Of chemical bonds,
And degraded health,
Now I have,
A life of wealth!

We have witnessed loss in *A Scary Dream*, and we saw change in *Transformations*. And we found a new beginning in the end, in *Vital Persistence*. New beginnings beyond loss and imagined ends.

"The perilous journeys,
I chose instinctively not to face,
Avoiding death,
Claiming life, in their place." — *Imagined Futures*

We will always find a way to go forward in life. There is always a new beginning.

"Humanity always,
Finds a way." — *Calculations*

Remember the past, love the past, take it with you when you go! Please don't leave it all behind. You would discard the meaning you have found in your life. Love what was, accept what is gone, and carry on. I know that it is easier said than done, but trying always helps.

"Flowers grow,
Around the memorial grave,
Remembrance." — *Transformations*

"I won't forget you,
But we need to move on,
Both of us,
Need to be strong." — *Birds Fly Away*

What would life be without loss? Would it be as beautiful or meaningful? We would certainly take it for granted until it is lost! I posit the same question for the people we love in our lives. What would life be like without having had them? Probably not as meaningful.

"I want to hold his friendly hands.
Share with him,
Successes,
Of life plans,
But his life ran out,
So many palms." — *One Day*

The beauty of this book for me is that the poems focus on specific topics, but if you sit with them, you can pull more insight and understanding from them. What meanings did you find? I hope what you gathered is beautiful and helpful! I leave you now with this new beginning in your life, while I make my way on my own journey.

"The time has come,
To meet his fate,
Last of all,
The peaceful, silent retreat." — *Peaceful, Silent Retreat*

My peaceful, silent retreat is the completion of this book. I poured a lot of emotion into this writing. It has been the culmination of many years of life experience and learning. This book will have given you insight into the not-so-quiet life I have lived. And have yet to live!

"I don't know where I came from,
Or where I will go…,
I'm at peace,
That I may never know!" — *The Wolf*

About the Author

John Liam Edward Anderson (Avarithia), originally from Northern Ireland, is a writer living in Donegal, Ireland. With a growing book collection and an ever-growing list of writing ideas. His reading interests include psychology, biology, Sci-fi, and mythology. A lover of music and movies. He continues to expand his knowledge in various areas to cement his writing career.